THIS CANDLEWICK BIOGRAPHY BELONGS TO:

No endeavor by man
    to rise into the air
        can succeed,
        and only fools would attempt it.

— CHARLES-AUGUSTIN DE COULOMB,
PHYSICIST AND ENGINEER, 1780

To the women in my family —
aeronauts, always, of buoyant grace.
M. C. S.

For my daughters, Ava and Molly.
The sky is the limit.
M. T.

Text copyright © 2017 by Matthew Clark Smith
Illustrations copyright © 2017 by Matt Tavares

First edition in this format 2019

Library of Congress Catalog Card Number 2017931493

ISBN 978-0-7636-7732-9 (hardcover)
ISBN 978-1-5362-0554-1 (reformatted hardcover)
ISBN 978-1-5362-0555-8 (reformatted paperback)

19 20 21 22 23 TLF 10 9 8 7 6 5 4 3 2

Printed in Dongguan, Guangdong, China

This book was typeset in Bulmer MT.
The illustrations were done in ink and watercolor.

Candlewick Press
99 Dover Street
Somerville, Massachusetts 02144

visit us at www.candlewick.com

Lighter than Air

Sophie Blanchard, the First Woman Pilot

MATTHEW CLARK SMITH

illustrated by MATT TAVARES

CANDLEWICK PRESS

❧ TABLE OF CONTENTS ❧

Chapter 1 8

Chapter 2 12

Chapter 3 18

Chapter 4 22

Chapter 5 26

Chapter 6 30

Author's Note 34

Illustrator's Note 36

Selected Bibliography 37

Index 38

Author and Illustrator Biographies 40

CHAPTER 1

It was November 1783. For months France had buzzed about the brothers Montgolfier and their mad dreams of floating bags in the sky. Now the moment had arrived. The brothers had painted their balloon in royal blue and decorated it with red draperies, golden eagles, and smiling portraits of the King. They lit the straw underneath, and the giant bag swelled with smoke and hot air. Two brave aeronauts climbed inside. They waved at the crowd. And then the handlers let go of the ropes.

The great marvel began to rise, as did a great gasp from the spectators. It trembled slightly as it was caught by the west wind. And to the roar of a half million voices below, it floated calmly out of sight, high above the rooftops of Paris.

CHAPTER 2

Sophie Armant was five when the men first flew.

Sophie heard the news in Trois-Canons, her sleepy village by the
sea, and her heart swelled and swelled. She ran along the shore, her
arms stretched out like wings, and watched the seabirds scatter. The
little sandpipers were plain and nervous on land, just as Sophie felt,
with her great fear of carriages and crowds. And yet in the air the shy
birds seemed like entirely different creatures. They danced through
the sky like clouds.

Oh, thought Sophie, *to fly like they do!*

Even as Sophie grew older, France remained mad for balloons. Fashionable ladies wore balloon-shaped hats. Families dined on balloon-painted plates. In newspaper cartoons, men blew themselves up with hot air and rose into the sky.

The balloonists were heroes. Most famous of all was the daredevil Jean-Pierre Blanchard. He and John Jeffries were the first men to cross the English Channel by balloon. They had to toss everything overboard to keep from crashing into the sea—even their trousers!—but they made it.

Sophie read everything she could about Blanchard and his fellow adventurers. And there was one thing she couldn't help noticing. All of the balloonists were men. The sky was no place for a woman, some said. It was too cold up there, the air too thin, the winds too fierce. Women were made of weaker stuff. Their place was on earth.

Deep in Sophie's windswept heart, she knew that couldn't be true.

CHAPTER 3

One day, Sophie went to one of Monsieur Blanchard's ballooning shows. Afterward, Blanchard noticed the odd little woman with the faraway eyes.

"Do you like the balloons, mademoiselle?" said he.

"I belong in one, m'sieur," said Sophie. Blanchard, startled, began to laugh. But then he saw the fire behind her words, and he knew at once that she was meant for the air.

They made an unusual couple, the streetwise old showman and the shy, bird-eyed little woman. But they shared something as wide and deep as the sky. Before long they were married, and Sophie Armant became Sophie Blanchard.

The first time Sophie left the ground with Jean-Pierre, she watched the earth fall slowly away. She felt the shudder of the shifting wind. She felt the air turn crisp and cold, like the first taste of fall. She saw birds fly beneath her, like fish beneath a boat. She watched the houses, the carriages, the crowds — so big, so loud, from below — shrink into harmless dolls.

CHAPTER 4

After flying twice with her husband, in 1805 Sophie decided to go up alone. No woman had attempted it before.

When news got out, there was quite a stir. People clucked their disapproval, as people do. But again Sophie's fear and doubt melted away as the wind carried her up, and she felt only a breathless thrill. The incomparable sensation, she called it.

Flight was as dangerous as it was thrilling. In 1808, during his fifty-ninth ascent, Jean-Pierre suffered a heart attack and fell from his balloon. After an agonizing year, he died from his injuries, and Sophie was left alone.

For a time she could not bear to think of ballooning. But one gusty day, as she watched the birds swooping and dancing, she felt the sky call to her again, and she knew she must return to it. From now on she would fly solo, the world's first woman pilot.

CHAPTER 5

Sophie began selling tickets to her ballooning shows, as Jean-Pierre had done, and people came by the thousands to see her. Quickly she learned how to make a living doing what she loved most.

Sophie's daring knew no bounds. More often than not she went up in little more than a hanging chair.

She went up by day, and she went up by night. One cold night over the Alps, her nose began to bleed, and icicles formed on her face.

She went up in good weather, and she went up in bad. Once over France, she crashed into a marsh in a storm and nearly drowned.

She went up high, and she went up even higher. Once she was forced to climb and climb to escape a sudden hailstorm. Finally she climbed so high that she passed out in the thin air. Down below, they gave her up for dead.

Fourteen hours later, she landed. She said it had been a pleasant nap.

CHAPTER 6

By this time, the bird woman, as she was known, was as famous as anyone in Europe. She was summoned to Paris by Emperor Napoleon himself. The imperial palace seemed like a million miles from her seaside village. Standing there in the throne room, she felt like the ugly duckling turned into a swan.

The Emperor named her Aeronaut of the Official Festivals, as well as Chief Air Minister of Ballooning.

When Napoleon got married, Sophie set off fireworks from her balloon as the crowds gasped and applauded.

When the Empress gave birth to a son, Sophie flew over Paris, tossing out leaflets to announce the good news.

From time to time, with the world laid out beneath her, Sophie would let her mind drift to the beach of her childhood. She saw herself chasing the little birds along the shore and then up, up, into the sky. Now, she realized, she had lifted the spirits of thousands along with her.

That old world, the one she now soared above, had fought for so long to put limits on women.

Yes, Sophie said to herself, with a smile. *There is a limit. And that limit is the sky.*

Author's Note

When the first unmanned hydrogen balloon was sent up from Paris in 1783 (just a few months before the manned flight described at the beginning of this book), the little "cloud in a bag" drifted toward a village several miles away, where it came to rest — and was torn to shreds by terrified villagers with pitchforks. This anecdote helps to show us how very different Sophie Blanchard's world was from our own, and how truly wondrous the exploits of the brave balloonists must have seemed at the time. It was an age before the skies had been mastered, and before the earth had been thoroughly charted from above; it was an age when each flight was a feat of cutting-edge technology, an exhibition of jaw-dropping magic, and a leap of faith into the unknown. I hope that in these pages I have captured some small amount of what Sophie called that "incomparable sensation."

I was forced to use my imagination in describing Sophie's childhood in particular, as history has preserved very little information about her early life.

Sadly, what is best known about Sophie is the story of her death. At the age of forty-one, for her sixty-seventh flight she ascended at night in a white dress and white plumed hat, intending to put on a fireworks show for a crowd in Paris. She mentioned before climbing into her craft that she was nervous, which struck her friends as unusual. Only minutes later, a wayward firework set fire to the balloon, and she was thrown to her death on the rooftops below. Some saw the tragedy as inevitable — "proof," as one man wrote, "that a woman in a balloon is either out of her element, or too high in it." But the long lineage of women aeronauts, pilots, and astronauts who followed Sophie, from Blanche Scott to Bessie Coleman to Sally Ride, has long since proved them wrong. For me, Sophie's spectacular accomplishments will always rise above her tragic end.

ILLUSTRATOR'S NOTE

When I first started working on this book, I spent a lot of time looking up at the sky. I tried to imagine how wondrous it must have seemed to Sophie when she was young. I started noticing things I hadn't noticed before: the way a few beams of sunlight would emerge from behind a dark cloud after a storm, or the way the clouds look almost otherworldly from the window seat of an airplane. I took hundreds of pictures. Sometimes I would notice an amazing cloud formation while driving, and I'd have to pull over. Once, when I was coaching first base during my daughter's little league game, the sun hit the clouds just right, and I had to sneak a few quick photos between pitches. In my illustrations, I tried to use the sky to help tell the story. When Sophie mourns, the sky is dark and ominous. In her moments of triumph, the sky is triumphant too. And in the end, when Sophie realizes the impact she has had on the world around her, the sky glows a warm yellow-orange. Because what could be more hopeful than the warm glow of the sun rising over the ocean at the beginning of a new day?

SELECTED BIBLIOGRAPHY

Darling, David. *The Rocket Man: And Other Extraordinary Characters in the History of Flight.* London: Oneworld, 2013.

Holmes, Richard. *Falling Upwards: How We Took to the Air.* New York: Pantheon, 2013.

Keen, Paul. "The 'Balloonomania': Science and Spectacle in 1780s England." *Eighteenth-Century Studies* 39, no. 4 (2006): 507–535.

Kotar, S. L., and J. E. Gessler. *Ballooning: A History, 1782–1900.* Jefferson, N. C.: McFarland, 2011.

Marion, Fulgence. *Wonderful Balloon Ascents: Or, The Conquest of the Skies.* New York: Scribner, 1870.

INDEX

Aeronaut of the Official
    Festivals, 30

aeronauts, 8–11, 35

Alps, 28

Armant, Sophie
    early interest in flying, 13, 17
    goes to Blanchard's
        ballooning show, 18
    marries Jean-Pierre
        Blanchard, 18
    See also Blanchard, Sophie

astronauts, women, 35

ballooning
    dangers, 24, 28–29
    early aeronauts, 8–11, 17
    English Channel
        crossing, 14
    first manned flight, 8–11

first unmanned hydrogen
    balloon, 34

popularity in France, 14

Blanchard, Jean-Pierre, 14
    death, 24
    first flight with Sophie,
        20–21
    marries Sophie Armant, 18

Blanchard, Sophie, 18
    crash, 28
    daring, 26–29
    death, 35
    and Emperor Napoleon, 30
    first solo flight, 22–23
    first flight with Jean-Pierre,
        20–21
    as first woman pilot, 25
    honors, 30
    Jean-Pierre's death, 24–25

known as bird woman, 30

makes living from
    ballooning, 25–30

passes out in thin air, 29

puts on ballooning
    shows, 26

sets off fireworks from
    balloon, 30–31

See also Armant, Sophie

Chief Air Minister of
    Ballooning, 30

Coleman, Bessie, 35

English Channel, 14

fireworks, 30–31, 35

France, 8–11, 14

hailstorm, 29

Jeffries, John, 14

Montgolfier brothers, 8–11

Napoleon (Emperor), 30

Paris, 10, 30, 34, 35

pilots, women, 35

Ride, Sally, 35

Scott, Blanche, 35

Trois-Canons, 13

women, 17, 25, 33, 35

MATTHEW CLARK SMITH has a master's degree in creative writing from Vermont College of Fine Arts. He lives in Crozet, Virginia.

MATT TAVARES has written and illustrated many books for kids, including *Zachary's Ball, Oliver's Game, Mudball, Henry Aaron's Dream, There Goes Ted Williams, Becoming Babe Ruth, Growing Up Pedro, Crossing Niagara,* and *Red and Lulu.* He lives in Ogunquit, Maine.